Do One Thing Every Morning to Make Your Day

A journal by:

I bid you the top of the mornin'.

John Locke

Are you the sort of person who wakes up at dawn and pops out of bed singing, "Oh, what a beautiful mornin'"? Or are you, instead, the person who clutches the sheets and growls through clenched teeth, "Oh! How I hate to get up in the morning"? In either case, this book will help you to enhance, expand, or change your outlook, and then set a positive direction for your day.

Do One Thing Every Morning to Make Your Day offers a wide array of quick activities to help you appreciate the magic of the morning and create effective rituals to jump-start days of health, energy, achievement, peace, goodness, and joy. Respond to the insights of writers, artists, entertainers, athletes, scientists, politicians, and philosophers. Be inspired by the real *Morning Routines* of modern and historical figures (including Benjamin Franklin's acts of goodness, Marie Kondo's tidying up, and Herman Melville's visits to his cow). In other repeating features you can become more intensely aware of the world inside or outside your window as you *Awaken Your Senses*. Or explore more deeply the familiar, as you M-E-D-I-T-A-T-E on your body, your morning shower, or even your coffee. Learn how to write a personal *Morning Affirmation*; remember to express your gratitude (*Thank You! Thank You! Thank You!*); and process your dreams through words and drawings (*Dream Catcher*). Choose a *Morning Stretch*—or two, or more—and try out some proven *Morning Tips* (from drinking warm lemon water to changing your waking time).

First thought, best thought.

Beat Generation motto

My first/best thought this morning:

_____

_____

_____

_____

_____

DATE: __ / __ / __

A NEW SIGHT THIS MORNING:

_____

_____

_____

_____

_____

_____

DATE: __ / __ / __

A NEW SOUND THIS MORNING:

_____

_____

_____

_____

_____

_____

Morning has broken,
Like the first morning.
Blackbird has spoken,
Like the first bird.

Eleanor Farjeon

A dream uninterpreted
is like a letter unopened.

Talmud

DATE: __ / __ / __

Draw a character, scene, or incident from last night's dream:

Dream Catcher

DATE: __ / __ / __

The meaning of my dream last night:

_____

_____

_____

_____

_____

_____

_____

_____

The first hour of the morning is the rudder of the day.

Henry Ward Beecher

How I set my course this morning:

_____

_____

_____

_____

_____

My future starts when I wake up in the morning and see the light.

Miles Davis

The future I see for myself in this morning's light:

_____

_____

_____

_____

_____

The goal of this yearlong exercise is to create a routine that suits you and inspires a sunny outlook for your day (see below and on the last page of this journal). Keep the book and a pen by your bed. Flip through the pages before you go to sleep or as soon as you wake up. Then follow the prompts in whatever order you like until, over the year, you have composed your perfect morning. Remember, though, that as you change and grow, your needs and preferences will change, too. When you are ready for something new, dive back in and reboot.

Now it is time to open your eyes and use the measure below. Then your adventures can begin.

DATE: __ / __ / __

MEASURE YOUR MORNINGS

How well do your early hours brighten your prospect for days of health, energy, achievement, peace, goodness, and joy?

Mark the brightness of your internal sun today.

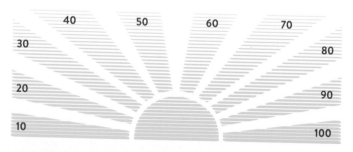

Think in the morning.
Act in the noon. Eat in the
evening. Sleep in the night.

William Blake

What I thought about this morning:

_____

_____

_____

_____

_____

Morning Tip:

Sip a cup of warm lemon water.

Warm lemon water first thing in the morning rehydrates your body, stimulates your digestive system, aids in detoxification, and supplies a dose of vitamin C.

☐ I did it this morning.

☐ I will add this to my morning routine.

Marmalade in the morning has the same effect on taste buds that a cold shower has on the body.

Jeanine Larmoth

_____ in the morning has the same effect on my

taste buds as a cold shower.

To wake at dawn with a winged heart and give thanks for another day of loving.

Kahlil Gibran

This morning I give thanks for loving _____.

"Oh, What a Beautiful Mornin'"

**Richard Rodgers and
Oscar Hammerstein II (song title)**

What is most beautiful about this mornin'?

☐ golden haze on the meadow

☐ corn as high as an elephant's eye

☐ sounds of the earth

☐ breeze in the trees

☐ something else: _____

DRAW YOURSELF BEFORE BREAKFAST:

DRAW YOURSELF AFTER BREAKFAST:

My general attitude toward life when I first get up is of deep suspicion. . . . I am simply basted together until after breakfast.

Gladys Taber

Morning

Create your own affirmation of health by using one of the adjectives below.

I, _____, am _____ and fueled
    your name   *adjective*   for the day.

energetic

strong

healthy

charged

vital

active

flexible

_____
other

Affirmation
HEALTH

DATE: __ / __ / __

Write your affirmation of health 5 times along this spiral.

All the really good ideas I ever had came to me while I was milking a cow.

Grant Wood

When I get my best morning ideas:

- ☐ brushing my teeth
- ☐ taking a shower
- ☐ making breakfast
- ☐ reading /listening to the news
- ☐ doing this chore: _____
- ☐ other: _____

THE MUSES LOVE THE MORNING.

Thomas Fuller

The inspiration I had this morning:

_____

_____

_____

_____

_____

MORNING ROUTINE

For the past 33 years, I have looked in the mirror every morning and asked myself: "If today were the last day of my life, would I want to do what I am about to do today?" And whenever the answer has been "No" for too many days in a row, I know I need to change something.

Steve Jobs

Look in the mirror and ask yourself Steve Jobs's question.
If the answer is no, what will you change?

_____

_____

_____

_____

To business that we love we rise betime, And go to't with delight.

William Shakespeare

The business that I rise and go to with delight:

_____

_____

_____

_____

_____

_____

_____

DATE: __ / __ / __

HOW THE COMMITTEE OF SLEEP RESOLVED A PERSONAL PROBLEM:

_____

_____

_____

_____

_____

_____

DATE: __ / __ / __

HOW THE COMMITTEE OF SLEEP RESOLVED A WORK PROBLEM:

_____

_____

_____

_____

_____

_____

It is a common
experience
that a problem
difficult at night
is resolved in
the morning after
the committee
of sleep has worked
on it.

John Steinbeck

Night is the mother of thoughts.

John Florio

A new thought I had on waking:

_____

_____

_____

_____

_____

MORNING IS WISER THAN EVENING.

Russian proverb

Wisdom that came to me this morning:

_____

_____

_____

_____

_____

MORNING STRETCH

FULL-LENGTH STRETCH

On your back in bed, inhale and hold your breath. Reach your arms overhead, linking your fingers together. Turn your palms outward and press them away from you. Meanwhile, stretch your legs and toes out as far as you can. Hold this position for 5 seconds; then exhale and release the stretch. Repeat 3 times.

☐ I did it this morning!

☐ I will do this again.

Getting fit is a political act—you are taking charge of your life.

Jane Fonda

After this morning's stretch, I believe I can take this on:

_____

_____

_____

_____

_____

_____

Morning is sweeter
For her voice.

Hilda Conkling

The first sweet voice of my morning:

_____

_____

_____

_____

_____

See in the east, th' illustrious king of day!
His rising radiance drives the shades
        away.

Phillis Wheatley

Draw the scene outside your window when you first open your eyes.

HE THAT WOULD
THRIVE
MUST RISE AT FIVE;
HE THAT HATH
THRIVEN
MAY LIE TILL
SEVEN.

John Clarke

DATE: __ / __ / __

TODAY I GOT UP AT 5:00 A.M. AND ACCOMPLISHED THIS:

_____

_____

_____

_____

_____

_____

DATE: __ / __ / __

TODAY I ALLOWED MYSELF TO SLEEP LATE BECAUSE I ACCOMPLISHED THIS YESTERDAY:

_____

_____

_____

_____

_____

_____

Awaken Your Senses:
Touch

The joyous morning ran and kissed
the grass
And drew his fingers through her
sleeping hair.

John Freeman

DATE: __ / __ / __

Describe the effect of the morning air on your skin:

_____

_____

_____

_____

_____

_____

DATE: __ / __ / __

Note your first touch of the morning:

☐ bedding

☐ floor

☐ person or pet

☐ cell phone

☐ _____
        other

Start every day off with a smile and get it over with.

W. C. Fields, attributed

What made me smile this morning:

_____

_____

_____

_____

_____

Make two grins grow where there was only a grouch before.

Elbert Hubbard

How I made someone smile with me this morning:

_____

_____

_____

_____

_____

Dream Catcher

The personal wish my heart made in my dream last night:

_____

_____

_____

_____

_____

_____

_____

_____

A Dream Is a Wish Your Heart Makes.

Walt Disney's "Cinderella" (song title)

DATE: __ / __ / __

The professional wish my heart made in my dream last night:

_____

_____

_____

_____

_____

_____

_____

Hello, sun in my face.
Hello, you who made
the morning
and spread it over
the fields. . . .
Watch, now, how
I start the day
in happiness,
in kindness.

Mary Oliver

DATE: __/__/__

A HAPPINESS TO START MY DAY:

_____

_____

_____

_____

_____

_____

DATE: __/__/__

A KINDNESS TO START MY DAY:

_____

_____

_____

_____

_____

_____

THE AMOUNT OF SLEEP REQUIRED BY THE AVERAGE PERSON IS ABOUT FIVE MINUTES MORE.

Max Kauffmann, attributed

The amount of sleep I require:

_____

_____

_____

The amount of sleep I got last night:

_____

_____

_____

Monday mornings were God's revenge.

Barbara Parker

How I cope with Monday mornings:

_____

_____

_____

_____

_____

_____

_____

Morning Tip:

Make your bed.

Whether you make a "military bed" with hospital corners or just pull up your duvet, this will start your day in a positive state of mind.

☐ I made my bed this morning.

☐ I will add this to my morning routine.

DATE: __ /__ /__

If you make your bed every morning, you will have accomplished the first task of the day. It will give you a small sense of pride, and it will encourage you to do another task and another and another.

Admiral William H. McRaven

After making my bed this morning, I completed

this task _____ and

this task _____ and

this task _____ .

DATE: __ / __ / __

'Tis always morning somewhere in the world.

Richard Henry Horne

Oops! I overslept this morning—it is _____:_____ A.M./P.M. here in

_____.

Fortunately it is only _____:_____ A.M. in _____.

Most people do not consider dawn to be an attractive experience— unless they are still up.

Ellen Goodman

How I spent my night on the town:

_____

_____

_____

How I feel about dawn this morning:

_____

_____

_____

DATE: __ / __ / __

I AM AWAKE TO THIS NEW RELATIONSHIP:

_____

_____

_____

_____

_____

_____

DATE: __ / __ / __

I AM AWAKE TO THIS NEW IDEA:

_____

_____

_____

_____

_____

_____

Only that day
dawns to which
we are awake.

Henry David Thoreau

Thank You!
Thank You!
Thank You!

I awoke this morning with devout
thanksgiving for my friends,
the old and the new.

Ralph Waldo Emerson

DATE: __ / __ / __

I awoke feeling grateful for this old friend:

_____

_____

_____

_____

_____

DATE: __ / __ / __

I awoke feeling grateful for this new friend:

_____

_____

_____

_____

_____

DATE: __ / __ / __

With the morning cool reflection came.

Sir Walter Scott

This morning's reflection:

_____

_____

_____

_____

_____

_____

_____

With the morning cool repentance came.

Sir Walter Scott

This morning's repentance:

_____

_____

_____

_____

_____

_____

_____

DATE: __/__/__

MORNING ROUTINE

Benjamin Franklin began his ideal daily routine by
recording the answer to this question:
"What good shall I do today?"

My answer to Franklin's question this morning:

_____

_____

_____

_____

_____

Good that comes late is good for nothing.

English proverb

A good deed I will do first thing this morning:

_____

_____

_____

_____

_____

Whether one is twenty, forty, or sixty; whether one has succeeded, failed, or just muddled along. . . . Life begins each morning! . . . Each morning is the open door to a new world—new vistas, new aims, new tryings.

Leigh Mitchell Hodges

DATE: __ / __ / __

THIS MORNING'S NEW VISTA:

_____

_____

_____

DATE: __ / __ / __

THIS MORNING'S NEW AIM:

_____

_____

_____

DATE: __ / __ / __

THIS MORNING'S NEW TRYING:

_____

_____

_____

When you do something beautiful
and nobody notices, do not be sad.
For the sun every morning is a beautiful
spectacle, and yet most of the audience
still sleeps.

John Lennon, attributed

☐ Today I woke in time for the spectacle of the sunrise.

I'll tell you how the Sun rose—
A Ribbon at a time.

Emily Dickinson

I'll tell you how the sun rose:

_____

_____

_____

_____

M-E-D-I-T-A-T-E:

Body Scan

Set a bell to ring in 3 minutes. Lie on your back in bed.
Close your eyes. Breathe in through your nose and out through your
mouth throughout this meditation. Relax your body, starting at the
top of your scalp and ending with the tips of your toes. As you scan
downward, briefly focus your breathing on areas of tightness;
then move on. When the bell rings, slowly open your eyes.

☐ I did it!

☐ How I feel:

_____

Meditation is the action of silence.

Jiddu Krishnamurti

How the silence acts on me as I meditate:

_____

_____

_____

_____

_____

_____

_____

Swallow a toad in the morning if you want to encounter nothing more disgusting the rest of the day.

Nicolas Chamfort

The "toad" I will swallow this morning:

_____

_____

_____

_____

_____

WHEN TWO PATHS OPEN BEFORE YOU, TAKE THE HARDER ONE.

Nepalese proverb

The harder path I will take this morning:

_____

_____

_____

_____

_____

DATE: __ / __ / __

MY NEW STRENGTH THIS MORNING:

_____

_____

_____

_____

_____

_____

DATE: __ / __ / __

MY NEW THOUGHTS THIS MORNING:

_____

_____

_____

_____

_____

_____

With the new day comes new strength and new thoughts.

Eleanor Roosevelt

Awaken Your Senses:
Sight

Beloved, it is morn!
A redder berry on the thorn,
A deeper yellow on the corn,
For this good day new-born.

Emily Henrietta Hickey

DATE: ___ / ___ / ___

Describe the colors of this morn:

_____

_____

_____

_____

_____

DATE: ___ / ___ / ___

Draw the sights of this morn from your window.

There is too much life to be lived for you to hit the snooze button. In fact, I believe it is "seize the day," not "snooze the day."

Hal Elrod

What I will seize today:

_____

_____

_____

_____

'Tis the voice of the sluggard,
I heard him complain,
"You have waked me too
soon, I must slumber again."

Isaac Watts

My excuse for being a sluggard:

_____

_____

_____

_____

_____

Dream Catcher

DATE: __ / __ / __

Last night I dreamt I went to _____ **again.**

Describe:

_____

_____

_____

_____

_____

_____

_____

Last night I dreamt I went to Manderley again.

Daphne du Maurier

DATE: __/__/__

Draw the place you visited in your dream last night.

I get up every morning determined to both change the world and have one hell of a good time. Sometimes this makes planning my day difficult.

E. B. White

DATE: __ / __ / __

HOW I WILL CHANGE THE WORLD TODAY:

_____

_____

_____

_____

_____

_____

DATE: __ / __ / __

HOW I WILL HAVE A GOOD TIME TODAY:

_____

_____

_____

_____

_____

THE WORLD IS ALWAYS YOUNG AGAIN FOR JUST A FEW MOMENTS AT THE DAWN.

L. M. Montgomery

How young I felt as I woke up this morning:

_____

_____

_____

_____

_____

IN OUR DREAMS, WE ARE ALWAYS YOUNG.

Sadie Delany

How young I was in last night's dream:

_____

_____

_____

_____

_____

Morning Tip:

Let the light in.

Turn on the lights or open the curtains as soon as you are up.
This signals your brain that it is time to wake up.

☐ I did it this morning.

☐ I will add this to my morning routine.

Behold how brightly breaks the morning!
Though bleak our lot, our hearts are warm.

James Kenney

The morning light warms my heart in spite of this concern:

_____

_____

_____

_____

_____

_____

Comrades, leave me here a little, while
as yet 'tis early morn:
Leave me here, and when you want me,
sound upon the bugle horn.

Alfred, Lord Tennyson

What woke me this morning:
- [ ] bugle horn
- [ ] alarm
- [ ] child
- [ ] my music
- [ ] someone else's music
- [ ] garbage truck
- [ ] other: _____

DATE: __/__/__

The happiest part of a man's life is what he passes lying awake in bed in the morning.

Samuel Johnson

My happy thoughts this morning lying in bed:

_____

_____

_____

_____

_____

DATE: __ / __ / __

HOW I WILL MAKE TODAY A HAPPY ONE FOR THIS FRIEND _____:

_____

_____

_____

_____

_____

_____

DATE: __ / __ / __

HOW I WILL MAKE TODAY A HAPPY ONE FOR THIS PERSON IN NEED

_____:

_____

_____

_____

_____

_____

_____

When you rise in the morning, form a resolution to make the day a happy one for a fellow creature.

Sydney Smith

Morning

Create your own affirmation of relationships by using one of the adjectives below.

I, _____, am _____ and can build strong
   your name   *adjective*
                                              connections with others.

compassionate

thoughtful

open

loving

honest

inspiring

responsive

_____
other

Affirmation
RELATIONSHIPS

DATE: __ / __ / __

Write your affirmation of relationships 5 times along these lines.

The supply of time is truly a daily miracle. . . . You wake up in the morning, and lo! your purse is magically filled with twenty-four hours of the unmanufactured tissue of the universe of your life! . . . It is the most precious of possessions.

Arnold Bennett

What I will do with my precious twenty-four hours from the moment I wake up:

_____

_____

_____

_____

_____

The morning has gold in its mouth.

German proverb

The gold I found in the mouth of this morning:

_____

_____

_____

_____

_____

MORNING ROUTINE

A big part of my morning routine is about what I don't do: when I wake up, I don't start my day by looking at my phone.

Arianna Huffington

What I *don't* do when I wake up in the morning:

_____

_____

_____

_____

_____

_____

ALMOST EVERYTHING WILL WORK AGAIN IF YOU UNPLUG IT FOR A FEW MINUTES, INCLUDING YOU.

Anne Lamott

How waking up without electronics reboots me:

_____

_____

_____

_____

_____

_____

I HAVE, ALL MY LIFE LONG, BEEN LYING TILL NOON; YET I TELL ALL YOUNG MEN, AND TELL THEM WITH GREAT SINCERITY, THAT NOBODY WHO DOES NOT RISE EARLY WILL EVER DO ANY GOOD.

Samuel Johnson

DATE: __/__/__

THIS MORNING I ROSE EARLY (__:__ A.M.) AND ACCOMPLISHED THIS:

_____

_____

_____

_____

_____

_____

DATE: __/__/__

THIS MORNING I LAY IN BED TILL NOON AND STILL ACCOMPLISHED THIS:

_____

_____

_____

_____

_____

_____

EVERY MORNING I GET UP AND LOOK THROUGH THE *FORBES* LIST OF THE RICHEST PEOPLE IN AMERICA. IF I'M NOT THERE, I GO TO WORK.

Robert Orben, attributed

What inspires me to go to work in the morning:

_____

_____

_____

_____

_____

Every morning I walk by a funeral home, and that's my productivity hack for how to make sure your to-do list is properly prioritized.

Anil Dash, attributed

This inspires me to properly prioritize my to-do list in the morning:

_____

_____

_____

_____

_____

MORNING STRETCH

HIP-THIGH-BUTT STRETCH

Lying on your back with your knees up, place your right ankle on your left knee. With your hands joined under your left thigh, press that knee toward your chest. Hold for 5 seconds. Then switch sides. Repeat 3 times.

☐ I did it this morning!

☐ I will do this again.

DATE: __/__/__

THE BODY SAYS WHAT
WORDS CANNOT.

Martha Graham

What my body is telling me this morning:

_____

_____

_____

_____

_____

_____

He instantly despised his guests for being still asleep, in a rush of that superiority which afflicts all those who are astir earlier than other people.

Vita Sackville-West

How I feel when I am astir while others are still sleeping:

_____

_____

_____

_____

_____

Up, sluggard, and waste not life; in the grave will be sleeping enough.

Benjamin Franklin

What life ambition got me up this morning:

_____

_____

_____

_____

_____

DATE: __ / __ / __

HOW I MADE MYSELF PLEASANT AT ___:___ A.M.

_____

_____

_____

_____

_____

_____

DATE: __ / __ / __

HOW I MADE MYSELF PLEASANT AT ___:___ A.M.

_____

_____

_____

_____

_____

_____

Be pleasant until
ten o'clock in
the morning and
the rest of the
day will take care
of itself.

Arthur Frederick Sheldon

Awaken Your Senses:
Hearing

Now the sun is rising calm and bright;
The birds are singing in the distant woods;
Over his own sweet voice the Stock-dove broods;
The Jay makes answer as the Magpie chatters;
And all the air is filled with pleasant noise of waters.

William Wordsworth

DATE: __/__/__

This morning the air is filled with the pleasant noises of:

_____

_____

_____

_____

_____

DATE: __/__/__

Note the first sounds you hear this morning:

☐ birds

☐ wind

☐ person

☐ traffic

☐ _____
other

Morning [is] a wonderful blessing, either sunny or stormy. It stands for hope . . . giving us another start of what we call "Life."

Horace Armour

My hope this morning:

_____

_____

_____

_____

_____

This is another day! And flushed
        Hope walks
Adown the sunward slopes with
        golden (shoes).

Don Marquis

My hope this morning:

_____

_____

_____

_____

_____

Dream Catcher

DATE: __ / __ / __

How my dream last night altered the color of my mind:

_____

_____

_____

_____

_____

_____

_____

_____

I've dreamt in my life dreams that have stayed
with me ever after, and changed my ideas:
they've gone through and through me, like
wine through water, and altered the colour
of my mind.

Emily Brontë

DATE: __ / __ / __

Describe or draw last night's dream.

There is no doubt that running away on a fresh, blue morning can be exhilarating.

Jean Rhys

DATE: __ / __ / __

WHY I WOULD RUN AWAY ON THIS FRESH, BLUE MORNING:

_____

_____

_____

_____

_____

_____

DATE: __ / __ / __

WHERE I WOULD RUN AWAY TO ON THIS FRESH, BLUE MORNING:

_____

_____

_____

_____

_____

_____

DATE: ___/___/___

Whether I retire to bed early or late, I rise with the sun.

Thomas Jefferson

I ☐ do ☐ do not imitate Jefferson because:

_____

_____

_____

_____

_____

The breeze at dawn has
secrets to tell you.
Don't go back to sleep.

Rumi

A secret the breeze told me at dawn today:

_____

_____

_____

_____

Morning Tip:

Eat a protein packed breakfast.

Protein gets you going.
Carbohydrates slow your body down.

My go-to protein-filled breakfast of champions:

_____

_____

☐ I added this to my daily routine.

Don't eat breakfast cereals that change the color of the milk.

Michael Pollan

Healthy grains I eat in the morning:

_____

_____

_____

_____

_____

Every morning upon awakening, I experience a supreme pleasure: that of being Salvador Dalí, and I ask myself, wonderstruck, what prodigious thing will he do today, this Salvador Dalí.

Salvador Dalí

What prodigious thing will this _____ do today?
                                        your name

_____

_____

_____

_____

_____

IT IS ODD HOW ONE CAN FEEL
LIKE SOMEONE ELSE EARLY IN THE
MORNING—BIGGER, CLEANER, SO
MUCH MORE ALIVE.

Maureen Daly

What my bigger, cleaner, much more alive self will try to accomplish
today:

_____

_____

_____

_____

_____

DATE: __ / __ / __

☐ I STARTED THE MORNING OFF WITH THIS SMILE IN THE MIRROR:

DATE: __ / __ / __

☐ I HAVE BEEN SMILING IN THE MIRROR EVERY MORNING FOR _____ DAYS.
THE BIG DIFFERENCE:

_____

_____

_____

_____

_____

Smile in the mirror. Do that every morning and you'll start to see a big difference in your life.

Yoko Ono, attributed

Thank You!
Thank You!
Thank You!

I feel very happy to see the sun come up every day. I feel happy to be around.... I like to take this day—any day—and go to town with it.

Jame Dickey

DATE: ___ / ___ / ___

I feel happy to be around this morning because:

_____

_____

_____

_____

_____

DATE: ___ / ___ / ___

How I will go to town with this day:

_____

_____

_____

_____

_____

Sadness flies on the wings of the morning—and out of the heart of darkness comes the light.

Jean Giraudoux

I woke up this morning with a renewed sense of happiness about:

_____

_____

_____

_____

_____

When that first cold, bright streak comes over the water, it's as if all our sins were pardoned; it's as if the sky leaned over the earth and kissed it and gave it absolution.

Willa Cather

This morning I woke up feeling forgiven for:

_____

_____

_____

_____

_____

MORNING ROUTINE

I rise at eight—thereabouts—& go to my barn—say good-morning to the horse, & give him his breakfast. . . . Then, pay a visit to my cow—cut up a pumpkin or two for her, & stand by to see her eat it. . . . My own breakfast over, I go to my work-room & light my fire—then spread my M.S.S. on the table—take one business squint at it, & fall to with a will.

Herman Melville

This morning routine gets me ready to fall to my work with a will:

_____

_____

_____

_____

_____

He who every morning plans
the transactions of the day and
follows out that plan, carries
on a thread which will guide him
through the labyrinth of the most
busy life.

Hugh Blair

The thread I will carry from this morning through the day:

_____

_____

_____

_____

_____

Every new day begins with possibilities; it's up to us to fill it with the things that move us toward progress and peace.

Ronald Reagan

DATE: __ / __ / __

HOW I WILL FILL TODAY WITH THINGS THAT MOVE THE WORLD TOWARD PROGRESS:

_____

_____

_____

_____

_____

DATE: __ / __ / __

HOW I WILL FILL TODAY WITH THINGS THAT MOVE THE WORLD TOWARD PEACE:

_____

_____

_____

_____

_____

Sometimes you climb out of bed in the morning and you think, *I'm not going to make it*, but you laugh inside . . . remembering all the times you've felt that way.

Charles Bukowski

I thought I couldn't make it this morning, but I remembered this:

_____

_____

_____

and laughed.

It's completely usual for me to get up in the morning, take a look around, and laugh out loud.

Barbara Kingsolver

Why I laughed out loud this morning:

_____

_____

_____

_____

DATE: __/__/__

M-E-D-I-T-A-T-E:

Seasons

Walk outside early in the morning for a seasonal meditation.
Notice the distinct colors around and above you. Focus on the light
passing through the trees, reflected on the water, on windows. Inhale
the special fragrances. Feel the dance of air on your skin. Listen for new
and familiar sounds. When your senses are fully engaged by the season,
return your focus inward, to your breath, and walk back inside.

☐ I did this in the _____.

season

☐ I will do this again ☐ soon ☐ in the _____.

season

I, singularly moved
To love the lovely that are not beloved,
Of all the Seasons, most
Love Winter.

Coventry Patmore

In the mornings, I love _____ most because:

this season

_____

_____

_____

_____

_____

_____

TO HAVE A REASON TO GET UP IN THE MORNING, IT IS NECESSARY TO POSSESS A GUIDING PRINCIPLE. A BELIEF OF SOME KIND. A BUMPER STICKER, IF YOU WILL.

Judith Guest

My bumper sticker this morning:

If there is anything that would kill me, it is to wake up in the morning not knowing what to do.

Nelson Mandela

What I will do today:

_____

_____

_____

_____

_____

DATE: __ / __ / __

HOW I PROCRASTINATED THIS MORNING:

_____

_____

_____

_____

_____

_____

DATE: __ / __ / __

ONLY THIS COULD MAKE ME WANT TO GET UP THIS MORNING:

_____

_____

_____

_____

_____

_____

"Oh! How I Hate to Get Up in the Morning"

Irving Berlin (song title)

Awaken Your Senses:
Smell

Sweet is the breath of the morn,
her rising sweet,
With charm of earliest birds.

John Milton

DATE: __ / __ / __

The sweet breath of this morning:

_____

_____

_____

_____

_____

DATE: __ / __ / __

Note the first scent of the morning:

☐ bacon

☐ coffee

☐ bread

☐ flowers

☐ _____
_ _other_

DATE: __/__/__

You haven't partied until you've partied at dawn in complete silence with Buddhist monks.

Cameron Diaz

How I partied at dawn with _____.

_____

_____

_____

_____

_____

As long as we live, there is never enough singing.

Martin Luther

What I sang in the shower this morning:

_____

_____

_____

_____

_____

Dream Catcher

What last night's dream communicated to me about myself:

_____

_____

_____

_____

_____

_____

_____

_____

Both dreams and myths are important communications from ourselves to ourselves.

Erich Fromm

Draw or describe the most mysterious scene in your dream last night. What might it mean?

So here hath been dawning
Another blue day:
Think, wilt thou
let it
Slip useless away?

Thomas Carlyle

DATE: __ / __ / __

I WILL USE TODAY TO ACCOMPLISH THIS:

_____

_____

_____

_____

_____

_____

DATE: __ / __ / __

I WILL USE TODAY TO CHANGE THIS:

_____

_____

_____

_____

_____

_____

It is by sitting down to write every morning that one becomes a writer.

Gerald Brenan

It is by sitting down to _____ every morning that

I can become a _____.

Not a day without a line.

Apelles

Start today by making a drawing with a continuous line:

Morning Tip:

Start your day earlier.

The best method for changing the time you wake up is to do it gradually—10 to 15 minutes earlier for 2 to 4 days, until you feel used to it. Then repeat until you reach your ideal wake-up time.

What I will do with my extra time:

_____

_____

_____

_____

My new wake-up time:

THE DARKEST HOUR IS JUST BEFORE DAWN.

American proverb

How the dawn lightened my spirits:

_____

_____

_____

_____

_____

Life always offers you a second chance, it's called tomorrow.

Nicholas Sparks, attributed

This morning I have a second chance to:

_____

_____

_____

_____

_____

DATE: __ / __ / __

OF ALL MORNING SMELLS, THE BEST IS:

_____

_____

_____

_____

_____

_____

DATE: __ / __ / __

OF ALL MORNING TASTES, THE BEST IS:

_____

_____

_____

_____

_____

_____

Of all smells,
bread: of all
tastes, salt.

George Herbert

Morning

DATE: __/__/__ Create your own affirmation for work by using one of the adjectives below.

I, _____, am _____ and can meet
   your name   *adjective*   the day's challenges.

confident

knowledgeable

capable

fair

persistent

articulate

inspiring

_____

other

Affirmation
WORK

DATE: __ / __ / __

Write your affirmation for work 5 times on this symbol for infinity.

Coffee should be black as hell, strong as death, and sweet as love.

Turkish proverb

I like my morning coffee _____,

_____,

and _____.

Peace, happiness, and joy is possible during the time I drink my tea.

Thich Nhat Hanh, attributed

_____,

_____,

and _____

are possible during the time I drink my morning tea.

MORNING ROUTINE

When I was young I started picking out my outfits
the night before school, and I still do this! I lay out
everything from my underwear to my jewelry. I also
pack my backpack and purse. This ritual gives me
a sense of tranquillity before bedtime.

Amanda Hesser

☐ I tried Amanda Hesser's routine.

It ☐ worked ☐ did not work for me this morning because:

_____

_____

_____

_____

_____

Each morning the day lies like a fresh shirt on our bed. . . . The happiness of the next twenty-four hours depends on our ability, on waking, to pick it up.

Walter Benjamin

What I did this morning that led to 24 hours of happiness:

_____

_____

_____

_____

_____

Each morning sees
some task begin,
Each evening
sees it close;
Something
attempted,
something done,
Has earned a
night's repose.

Henry Wadsworth Longfellow

DATE: __ / __ / __

THE TASK I WILL BEGIN THIS MORNING:

_____

_____

_____

_____

_____

_____

DATE: __ / __ / __

THE ATTEMPT I WILL MAKE THIS MORNING:

_____

_____

_____

_____

_____

_____

It is a visual joy to watch
light turn to color by

Draw the early morning grays.

the grays in the morning

the sun. ◀ Jo Scott-B

DATE: __ /__ /__

Draw the same scene colored by the sun.

MORNING STRETCH

BACK STRETCH

Hang your legs over the side of your bed or sit in a chair, making sure that your feet touch the ground. Lean forward and round your back, hanging your head and arms toward the floor. Take five deep breaths in and out.

☐ I did it this morning!

☐ I will do this again.

IT IS REMARKABLE HOW ONE'S WITS ARE SHARPENED BY PHYSICAL EXERCISE.

Pliny the Younger

Proof that my wits were sharpened by my stretch this morning:

_____

_____

_____

_____

_____

MORNING PERSPECTIVE: IMAGINATION.

Ralph Waldo Emerson

What I imagined when I first woke up:

_____

_____

_____

_____

_____

It often happens that I wake at night and begin to think about a serious problem and decide I must tell the pope about it. Then I wake up completely and remember that I am the pope!

Pope John XXIII

When I woke up completely this morning, I remembered that:

_____

_____

_____

_____

DATE: __ / __ / __

I GOT UP IN THE MORNING LOOKING FOR THIS PERSONAL ADVENTURE:

_____

_____

_____

_____

_____

_____

DATE: __ / __ / __

I GOT UP IN THE MORNING LOOKING FOR THIS PROFESSIONAL ADVENTURE:

_____

_____

_____

_____

_____

_____

I get up in
the morning
looking for
an adventure.

George Foreman

Awaken Your Senses:
Taste

When one has tasted [watermelon],
he knows what the angels eat.

Mark Twain

DATE: ___ /___ /___

What I think the angels eat for breakfast:

_____

_____

_____

_____

DATE: ___ /___ /___

Note your first taste of the morning:

☐ coffee/tea

☐ juice

☐ jam

☐ watermelon

☐ _____
other

I have nothing against mornings.
Both sunrises I've personally
witnessed were no less than
spectacular.

Suzann Ledbetter

This morning I ☐ saw the sunrise.

☐ slept late.

How I feel:

_____

_____

_____

_____

_____

There's a sunrise and a sunset every single day, and they're absolutely free. Don't miss so many of them.

Jo Walton

Draw the sunrise this morning. Priceless!

Dream Catcher

DATE: ___/___/___

The romantic dream I had last night:

_____

_____

_____

_____

_____

_____

_____

_____

I do not understand the capricious lewdness of the sleeping mind.

John Cheever

DATE: __ / __ / __

Write an interpretation of your dream last night.

_____

_____

_____

_____

_____

_____

_____

**EVERY DAY, THINK
AS YOU WAKE UP:
TODAY I AM FORTUNATE
TO BE ALIVE, I HAVE
A PRECIOUS HUMAN
LIFE, I AM NOT GOING
TO WASTE IT.**

Dalai Lama, attributed

DATE: ___/___/___

HOW I WILL USE MY PRECIOUS LIFE TO DEVELOP MYSELF TODAY:

_____

_____

_____

_____

_____

_____

DATE: ___/___/___

HOW I WILL USE MY PRECIOUS LIFE TO BENEFIT OTHERS TODAY:

_____

_____

_____

_____

_____

_____

Every day is great— it's a day extra.

Jake LaMotta

What I will do with my extra day:

_____

_____

_____

_____

_____

Every morning, I wake up saying, "I'm still alive—a miracle." And so I keep on pushing.

Jacques Cousteau, attributed

What I will push for this morning:

_____

_____

_____

_____

DATE: __/__/__

Morning Tip:

Set your morning schedule.

Make a schedule for your morning activities. Select from these and number them. There is no right or wrong; just include what works for you:

- [ ] stretch
- [ ] exercise
- [ ] give thanks
- [ ] meditate
- [ ] work on a passion project

- [ ] make the bed
- [ ] affirm yourself
- [ ] record your dream
- [ ] awaken your senses
- [ ] eat a protein for breakfast

- [ ] care for your body
- [ ] set a daily goal
- [ ] _____
  other

A schedule defends from chaos and whim.

Annie Dillard

This morning I integrated this new element into my routine:

_____;

and/or eliminated this old one: _____.

DATE: ___/___/___

Sometimes I've believed as many as six impossible things before breakfast.

Lewis Carroll

Impossible things that I believed before breakfast this morning:

_____

_____

_____

_____

_____

_____

The brain is a wonderful organ;
it starts working the moment you
get up in the morning and does
not stop until you get into the office.

Robert Frost

My IQ when I woke up:

_____

_____

My IQ at the office:

_____

_____

DATE: __ / __ / __

MY FRESH TRY THIS MORNING:

_____

_____

_____

_____

_____

_____

DATE: __ / __ / __

MY ONE MORE START THIS MORNING:

_____

_____

_____

_____

_____

_____

I have always
been delighted at the
prospect of a new
day, a fresh try,
one more start, with
perhaps a bit of
magic waiting
somewhere behind
the morning.

J. B. Priestley

Thank You!

Thank You!

Thank You!

The early morning hour should be
dedicated to praise.
Do not the birds set us the
example?

Charles Spurgeon

DATE: __/__/__

This morning I gave praise for _____ in nature.

DATE: __/__/__

This morning I gave praise for _____ in my life.

YOU'VE GOT TO GET UP EVERY MORNING WITH DETERMINATION IF YOU'RE GOING TO GO TO BED WITH SATISFACTION.

George Horace Lorimer

This morning I woke up determined to:

_____

_____

_____

_____

_____

THERE'S THAT MOMENT EVERY MORNING WHEN YOU LOOK IN THE MIRROR: ARE YOU COMMITTED, OR ARE YOU NOT?

LeBron James

When I looked in the mirror this morning, I ☐ saw ☐ did not see commitment to:

_____

_____

_____

_____

_____

DATE: __/__/__

MORNING ROUTINE

I go to sleep promptly when I go to bed. Then I wake up around 4 and can't sleep. But my mind's clear, so I get up and work for three or four hours. Then I go to bed for another nap.

Frank Lloyd Wright

The hours when my mind is clearest:

_____

_____

_____

_____

_____

Mornings belong to whatever is new. . . . Afternoons are for naps and letters.

Stephen King

My morning belongs to this new project:

_____

_____

_____

_____

_____

Social action gives the imagination a reason to get up in the morning.

Pope. L

DATE: ___ / ___ / ___

SOCIAL ACTION I WILL TAKE FOR MY COMMUNITY TODAY:

_____

_____

_____

_____

_____

_____

DATE: ___ / ___ / ___

SOCIAL ACTION I WILL TAKE FOR THE WORLD TODAY:

_____

_____

_____

_____

_____

There is a sort of elation about sunlight and the upper part of a house.

Edward Hopper

Draw morning sunlight hitting a house or another object.

Flames in the forehead of the morning sky.

John Milton

Use a metaphor to describe this morning's sunrise:

_____

_____

_____

_____

_____

_____

_____

M-E-D-I-T-A-T-E:

Shower

Standing in the shower, feel the water hit your head, your shoulders, your trunk, your legs, your feet. Focus first on the temperature; next on the pressure as the jets of water strike you and bounce off. Rub on soap deliberately, noticing how it slides along the curves of your body. After you turn off the shower, stand for a moment, feeling the drops fall downward.

☐ I did it!

☐ How I feel:

_____

Meditation and water are wedded forever.

Herman Melville

How I meditated in a morning mist or rain today:

_____

_____

_____

_____

_____

_____

_____

Arranging a bowl of flowers in the morning can give a sense of quiet in a crowded day—like writing a poem, or saying a prayer.

Anne Morrow Lindbergh

Arranging flowers this morning made me feel:

_____

_____

_____

_____

_____

A morning glory at my window satisfies me more than the metaphysics of books.

Walt Whitman

A _____ at my window makes me feel:

_____

_____

_____

_____

_____

DATE: ___/___/___

LAST NIGHT'S DREAM TOLD ME THIS, WHICH I WISH:

_____

_____

_____

DATE: ___/___/___

LAST NIGHT'S DREAM TOLD ME THIS, WHICH I FEAR:

_____

_____

_____

DATE: ___/___/___

LAST NIGHT'S DREAM TOLD ME THIS, WHICH I ☐ DID KNOW ☐ DID NOT KNOW:

_____

_____

_____

Some dreams tell us what we wish to believe. Some dreams tell us what we fear. Some dreams are of what we know though we may not know we knew it. The rarest dream is the dream that tells us what we did not know.

Ursula K. Le Guin

Awaken Your Senses:
Touch

I perfectly feel, even at my finger's end.

John Heywood

DATE: ___ / ___ / ___

My most intense tactile sensation this morning:

_____

_____

_____

_____

DATE: ___ / ___ / ___

My most pleasurable tactile sensation this morning:

_____

_____

_____

_____

I like breakfast-time better than any other moment in the day. No dust has settled on one's mind then, and it presents a clear mirror to the rays of things.

George Eliot

What became clear to me at breakfast-time this morning:

_____

_____

_____

_____

_____

You can be passionate about anything. . . . Pay attention, don't let life go by you. Fall in love with the back of your cereal box.

Jerry Seinfeld

What impassioned me at breakfast-time this morning:

_____

_____

_____

_____

_____

Dream Catcher

How old I was in my dream last night:

_____

_____

_____

_____

_____

_____

_____

_____

In a dream you are never eighty.

Anne Sexton

DATE: __ / __ / __

What I looked like in my dream last night (draw or describe):

In winter, I get up
at night
And dress by yellow
candle-light.
In summer, quite
the other way,
I have to go to bed
by day.

Robert Louis Stevenson

DATE: __ /__ /__

A SPECIAL FEATURE OF MY WINTER MORNING RITUAL:

_____

_____

_____

_____

_____

_____

DATE: __ /__ /__

A SPECIAL FEATURE OF MY SUMMER MORNING RITUAL:

_____

_____

_____

_____

_____

Optimism is a moral choice. I wake up every day and choose to be optimistic.

Chelsea Clinton

When I woke up this morning, I chose to be optimistic about:

_____

_____

_____

_____

_____

DATE: __/__/__

Each day the world is born anew for him who takes it rightly.

James Russell Lowell

For me the world is new this morning, so I can:

_____

_____

_____

_____

_____

Morning Tip:

Put all electronics out of reach.

You will have to get out of bed to turn off the alarm, and you won't
be awakened by morning messages and texts.

This is where I keep my alarm:

_____

_____

_____

I saw something stupid in the paper today—a new alarm clock that makes no noise. It's for people who don't like loud noises. Instead, it slowly hits you with light and gets brighter and brighter until you wake up. I already have one of those . . . it's called a window.

Jay Leno

How I woke up without an alarm this morning:

_____

_____

_____

I fear waking up one morning and finding out my life was all for nothing. We're here for a reason. I believe a bit of the reason is to throw little torches out to lead people through the dark.

Whoopi Goldberg

This morning I will throw out this little torch:

_____

_____

_____

_____

Far away there in the sunshine are my highest aspirations.

Louisa May Alcott

What I will aspire to this morning:

_____

_____

_____

_____

_____

DATE: ___ / ___ / ___

THIS MORNING I AM WILLING TO BEGIN THIS NEW PROJECT:

_____

_____

_____

_____

_____

_____

DATE: ___ / ___ / ___

THIS MORNING I AM WILLING TO BEGIN THIS NEW RELATIONSHIP:

_____

_____

_____

_____

_____

_____

Be willing to
be a beginner
every single
morning.

Anonymous

Morning

DATE: ___ / ___ / ___

Create your personal affirmation by using one of the adjectives listed below.

I, _____ , am _____ and comfortable
        your name   *adjective*   in my skin.

self-aware

confident

understood

secure

wise

beloved

self-accepting

_____
other

Affirmation
SELF

DATE: __ / __ / __

Write your personal affirmation 5 times along these smiles.

NOTHING HAPPENS UNLESS FIRST A DREAM.

Carl Sandburg

My dream this morning:

_____

_____

_____

How I will make it real:

_____

_____

_____

Dreams reflect current and future unsolved problems and rehearse their possible solutions.

Alfred Adler

How a problem was solved in last night's dream:

_____

_____

_____

_____

_____

_____

_____

_____

MORNING ROUTINE

I like to get up when the dawn comes. The dogs start talking to me and I like to make a fire and maybe some tea and then sit in bed and watch the sun come up. The morning is the best time, there are no people around. My pleasant disposition likes the world with nobody in it.

Georgia O'Keeffe

In the morning my disposition likes the world with:

_____

_____

_____

_____

_____

DATE: __ / __ / __

Heaven to be the first one up and to eat breakfast all alone.

Katharine Hepburn

I prefer to have breakfast

☐ alone.

☐ with

_____.

AN EARLY MORNING WALK IS A BLESSING FOR THE WHOLE DAY.

Henry David Thoreau

DATE: __ / __ / __

MY FAMILIAR EARLY MORNING WALK TO _____
MADE ME FEEL BLESSED BECAUSE:

_____

_____

_____

_____

_____

DATE: __ / __ / __

MY UNFAMILIAR EARLY MORNING WALK TO _____
MADE ME FEEL BLESSED BECAUSE:

_____

_____

_____

_____

_____

Typically speaking, I'm happiest, smartest, most creative, and most optimistic between the hours of 4:00 and 8:00 A.M.

Scott Adams

Typically speaking, I am most _____

between the hours of 4:00 and 8:00 A.M.

When I'm ironing [before 7:30 A.M.], that's when I do most of my work.

George Balanchine

When I do most of my work:

_____

_____

_____

_____

_____

MORNING STRETCH

KNEE HUG

Lie on your back with your knees bent and feet flat on the bed. Bring your knees, one at a time, toward your chest and wrap your arms around your shins. Hold this position as you take 10 deep breaths, in and out. Release your legs slowly, one at a time.

☐ I did it this morning!

☐ I will do this again.

DATE: __ / __ / __

WE SHOULD CONDUCT OURSELVES NOT AS IF WE OUGHT TO LIVE FOR THE BODY, BUT AS IF WE COULD NOT LIVE WITHOUT IT.

Seneca the Younger

What I did to care for my body this morning:

_____

_____

_____

_____

_____

_____

Lose an hour in the morning, and you will be all the day hunting it.

Richard Whately, attributed

Oops! I overslept this morning. What I will never get around to doing:

_____

_____

_____

_____

_____

Rise an hour, an hour and a half, or even two hours earlier; and—if you must—retire earlier when you can. . . . You will accomplish as much in one morning hour as in two evening hours.

Arnold Bennett

The extra things I accomplished by rising _____ hour(s) earlier:

_____

_____

_____

_____

_____

DATE: __ / __ / __

A CHANGE IN MY ROUTINE WHEN I AM _____:
where

_____

_____

_____

DATE: __ / __ / __

A CHANGE IN MY ROUTINE WHEN I AM _____:
who

_____

_____

_____

DATE: __ / __ / __

A CHANGE IN MY ROUTINE WHEN I AM _____:
doing what

_____

_____

_____

I love the idea of a single, perfect, infallible morning routine, and I'm always searching for it, but unfortunately I have yet to find it. Meanwhile, I have several routines, which I'm always changing and which vary depending on where I am, who I am, and what I'm doing.

Ruth Ozeki

Awaken Your Senses:
Sight

All they could see was sky, water, birds, light, and confluence. It was the whole morning world.

Eudora Welty

DATE: __ / __ / __

My whole morning world:

_____

_____

_____

_____

_____

DATE: __ / __ / __

Use one word to describe your first sights of the morning:

☐ sky: _____

☐ water: _____

☐ birds: _____

☐ light: _____

☐ _____
other

If each of us works toward making a sincere effort when we wake up each morning with a renewed commitment and dedication to embracing nonviolence as a lifestyle, the world will become a better place, bringing us closer to the Beloved Community of which my father so often spoke.

Bernice King, attributed

My effort this morning to make the world a better place:

_____

_____

_____

_____

_____

Don't judge each day by the harvest you reap but by the seeds that you plant.

Robert Louis Stevenson

Seeds of goodness I will plant this morning:

_____

_____

_____

_____

_____

Dream Catcher

My morning dream, which showed me a truth about myself:

_____

_____

_____

_____

_____

_____

_____

Those dreams are true which we have in the morning.

Ovid

DATE: __ / __ / __

My morning dream, which showed me a truth about my work:

_____

_____

_____

_____

_____

_____

_____

_____

It is a good morning exercise for a research scientist to discard a pet hypothesis every day before breakfast.

Konrad Lorenz

DATE: __ / __ / __

A PET HYPOTHESIS ABOUT MYSELF THAT I DISCARDED THIS MORNING:

_____

_____

_____

_____

_____

_____

DATE: __ / __ / __

A PET HYPOTHESIS ABOUT THE WORLD THAT I DISCARDED THIS MORNING:

_____

_____

_____

_____

_____

_____

I like to wake each morning and not know what I think, that I may reinvent myself in some way.

Stephen Fry

How I will reinvent myself this morning:

_____

_____

_____

_____

_____

That leap up of the sun is as glad as a child's laugh; it is as a renewal of the world's youth.

Margaret Wade Campbell Deland

Why I felt glad this morning to wake up with the sun:

_____

_____

_____

_____

_____

DATE: ___/___/___

Morning Tip:

Exercise.

Working out in the morning can give you an energy boost, increase your mental focus, brighten your mood, and reduce stress. Researchers have also found that morning exercise can reduce blood pressure.

☐ I did these exercises this morning:

_____

_____

_____

☐ I will add exercise to my morning routine.

I don't count my sit-ups; I only start counting when it starts hurting . . . because then it really counts.

▲
Muhammad Ali
▼

Number of _____s
I did that counted this morning:

_____

_____

_____

_____

_____

This is a wonderful day. I've never seen this one before.

Maya Angelou

Why I think this day will be wonderful:

_____

_____

_____

_____

_____

BLISS WAS IT IN THAT DAWN TO BE ALIVE.

William Wordsworth

Why I feel blissful this morning:

_____

_____

_____

_____

_____

What I know for sure is that every day brings a chance for you to draw in a breath, kick off your shoes, and step out and dance—to live free of regret and filled with as much joy, fun, and laughter as you can stand.

Oprah Winfrey

DATE: __ / __ / __

HOW I WILL STEP OUT AND DANCE TODAY:

_____

_____

_____

_____

_____

_____

DATE: __ / __ / __

HOW I WILL FILL MY DAY WITH JOY, FUN, AND LAUGHTER:

_____

_____

_____

_____

_____

_____

Thank You!
Thank You!
Thank You!

When I started counting
my blessings, my whole life
turned around.

Willie Nelson

DATE: __ / __ / __

This morning I counted these blessings I have:

1. _____

2. _____

3. _____

4. _____

5. _____

DATE: __ / __ / __

This morning I counted these blessings I shared:

1. _____

2. _____

3. _____

4. _____

5. _____

I don't need an alarm clock. My ideas wake me.

Ray Bradbury

The idea that woke me up this morning:

_____

_____

_____

_____

_____

It is always with excitement that I wake up in the morning wondering what my intuition will toss up to me, like gifts from the sea. I work with it and rely on it. It's my partner.

Jonas Salk, attributed

This morning's intuition:

_____

_____

_____

_____

_____

MORNING ROUTINE

My five-year-old son wakes me up at 6:30 or 7:00 A.M. . . .
After playing with [him] for about an hour or so,
I get dressed. . . . If I don't get a chance to play with
my son in the morning I feel like I missed something
that I'll never get back. It's such a joy to wake up and
be in the mind-set of a five-year-old before transitioning
into the role of "executive."

Biz Stone

What puts me in a nonbusiness mind-set in the morning:

_____

_____

_____

_____

_____

How to become a morning person: live with a baby.

Jean Hsu

How my morning routine changed when I lived with

☐ a baby:

_____

_____

☐ a significant other:

_____

_____

☐ a pet:

_____

_____

LET EVERY DAWN OF MORNING BE TO YOU AS THE BEGINNING OF LIFE.

John Ruskin

DATE: __ / __ / __

I WILL BEGIN THIS NEW WORK PROJECT THIS MORNING:

_____

_____

_____

_____

_____

_____

DATE: __ / __ / __

I WILL BEGIN THIS NEW WORK ON MYSELF THIS MORNING:

_____

_____

_____

_____

_____

_____

TODAY IS THE DAY IN WHICH TO ATTEMPT AND ACHIEVE SOMETHING WORTHWHILE.

Grenville Kleiser, attributed

My worthwhile goal for today:

_____

_____

_____

_____

_____

ALL THE SPEED IS IN THE MORNING.

Alice Harvey

My speed this morning: _____ per hour

M-E-D-I-T-A-T-E:

Sunrise

Before daybreak, walk to a quiet spot. Sit comfortably, facing east, and feel the cool morning air enter your body as you breathe in and out. As the sky becomes brighter, close your eyes and lower your head, experiencing the sunrise through your eyelids. Imagine the light flowing down through your body from the top of your head. Once the sun has completely risen, return your focus to your breath, open your eyes, stand, and walk back.

☐ I did it!

☐ How I feel:

_____

For yesterday is but a dream
And tomorrow is only a vision
But today, well lived,
Makes every yesterday
a dream of happiness
And every tomorrow a vision of hope.
Look well, therefore, to this day!

**Salutation of the Dawn
(from the Sanskrit)**

How I will live well today:

_____

_____

_____

_____

_____

Day's sweetest moments are at dawn.

Ella Wheeler Wilcox

My sweetest moment this dawn:

_____

_____

_____

_____

_____

There in the windy flood of morning
Longing lifted its weight from me,
Lost as a sob in the midst of cheering,
Swept as a sea-bird out to sea.

Sara Teasdale

Why this morning gave me relief:

_____

_____

_____

_____

_____

DATE: __ / __ / __

WHAT IS TODAY'S MIRACLE?

_____

_____

_____

_____

_____

_____

DATE: __ / __ / __

WHAT IS TODAY'S MIRACLE?

_____

_____

_____

_____

_____

_____

You can become
blind by seeing each
day as a similar one.
Each day is a different
one, each day brings
a miracle of its own.
It's just a matter of
paying attention to
this miracle.

Paulo Coelho

Awaken Your Senses:
Hearing

Far off I hear the crowing of the cocks,
And through the opening door that time unlocks
Feel the fresh breathing of To-morrow creep.

Henry Wadsworth Longfellow

DATE: __ / __ / __

The sound that opened the door to morning:

_____

_____

_____

_____

_____

DATE: __ / __ / __

My morning playlist:

_____

_____

_____

_____

_____

HOPE IS A GOOD BREAKFAST.

Sir Francis Bacon, attributed

My hope this morning:

_____

_____

_____

_____

_____

I get up every morning and it's going to be a great day. You never know when it's going to be over so I refuse to have a bad day.

Paul Henderson

Today is going to be a great day because:

_____

_____

_____

_____

_____

Dream Catcher

DATE: __ / __ / __

Describe what you saw more clearly in your dream last night.

_____

_____

_____

_____

_____

_____

_____

_____

Why does the eye see a thing more clearly in dreams than with the imagination being awake?

Leonardo da Vinci

DATE: __ / __ / __

Draw something you saw more clearly in your dream last night.

I wake up every morning thinking . . . this is my last day. And I jam everything into it. There's no time for mediocrity. This is no damned dress rehearsal. You've got one life, so just lead it. And try to be remarkable.

Anita Roddick

DATE: __ / __ / __

WHAT I WILL JAM IN TODAY:

_____

_____

_____

_____

_____

_____

DATE: __ / __ / __

HOW I WILL TRY TO BE REMARKABLE TODAY:

_____

_____

_____

_____

_____

_____

People don't realize, how important it is to wake up every morning with a song in your heart.

Jiddu Krishnamurti, attributed

The song in my heart this morning:

_____

_____

_____

_____

_____

Dance, creature! Put down your pen, lift up your limbs, and dance to greet another golden morning.

Woody Harrelson

When I did my happy dance this morning:

_____

_____

_____

_____

_____

DATE: __/__/__

Morning Tip:

Keep a gratitude journal.

Writing down at least three things you are thankful for each morning will give you positive energy for the day and put in perspective your personal and professional concerns.

☐ I did it.

☐ I will add this to my morning routine.

Write it on your heart that every day is the best day of the year.

Ralph Waldo Emerson

Why today will be the best day of the year:

_____

_____

_____

_____

_____

Full many a glorious morning have I seen
Flatter the mountain-tops with sovereign eye,
Kissing with golden face the meadows green,
Gilding pale streams with heavenly alchemy.

William Shakespeare

Describe or draw a summer morning.

The icicles at dawn this morning were the color of opals—blue lit with fire.

Katherine Mansfield

Describe or draw a winter morning.

DATE: __ / __ / __

THIS MORNING I DREAM THAT I CAN:

_____

_____

_____

_____

_____

_____

DATE: __ / __ / __

THIS MORNING I BELIEVE THAT I CAN:

_____

_____

_____

_____

_____

_____

To accomplish
great things
we must not only
act, but also dream;
not only plan, but
also believe.

Anatole France

Morning

DATE: ___/___/___

Create your own personal affirmation of community by using one of the adjectives below.

I, _____, am _____ and can make
your name   *adjective*   the world better.

generous

inclusive

informed

compassionate

helpful

thoughtful

engaged

_____

other

Affirmation
COMMUNITY

DATE: __ / __ / __

Write your personal affirmation of community 5 times around this globe.

Yosemite Valley, to me, is always a sunrise, a glitter of green and golden wonder in a vast edifice of stone and space.

Ansel Adams

What is always a sunrise to me:

_____

_____

_____

_____

_____

I don't ask for the meaning of the song of a bird or the rising of the sun on a misty morning. There they are, and they are beautiful.

Pete Hamill

What is beautiful to me this morning:

_____

_____

_____

_____

_____

MORNING ROUTINE

I wake up around 6:30 in the morning. I open the windows to let in some fresh air, and I purify the house by burning incense. I like to have warm drinks like hot water or herbal tea before I eat breakfast. . . . [If] I have to leave the house before I have finished tidying perfectly . . . it's on my mind the whole day.

Marie Kondo

Tidying ☐ is ☐ is not part of my morning routine.
My tidying routine:

_____

_____

_____

_____

Routine is liberating. It makes you feel in control.

Carol Shields

This part of my morning routine makes me feel most in control:

_____

_____

_____

_____

_____

_____

_____

MORNING IS WONDERFUL. ITS ONLY DRAWBACK IS THAT IT COMES AT SUCH AN INCONVENIENT TIME OF DAY.

Glen Cook

DATE: __ / __ / __

INCONVENIENT TIME FOR MORNING TO COME:

_____

_____

_____

_____

_____

_____

DATE: __ / __ / __

CONVENIENT TIME FOR MORNING TO COME:

_____

_____

_____

_____

_____

_____

Swallow all your learning in the morning.

Lord Chesterfield

Something new I learned this morning:

_____

_____

_____

_____

_____

Never be afraid to sit awhile and think.

Lorraine Hansberry

This morning I sat in bed and thought about:

_____

_____

_____

_____

_____

MORNING STRETCH

SPINE TWIST

Lie on your back with your knees bent and feet flat on the bed. Draw both knees, one at a time, toward your chest, wrapping your arms around them. Keeping your knees bent and your shoulders on the mattress, spread your arms wide and drop your legs to the right. Then turn your face to the left. Take 10 deep breaths. Repeat in the other direction.

☐ I did it this morning!

☐ I will do this again.

I BELIEVE THAT THE PHYSICAL IS THE GEOGRAPHY OF THE BEING.

Louise Nevelson

How I feel this morning after stretching:

_____

_____

_____

_____

_____

_____

All memorable events . . . transpire in morning time and in a morning atmosphere.

Henry David Thoreau

A memorable event that transpired this morning:

_____

_____

_____

_____

_____

I don't grasp things this early in the day. I mean, I hear voices, all right, but I can't pick out the verbs.

Jean Kerr

I woke up at ___:___ A.M. this morning.

I felt

☐ groggy

☐ foggy

☐ hungover

☐ sharp

☐ alert

☐ _____

other

DATE: __ / __ / __

I AWAKENED TO THIS KNOWLEDGE OF MYSELF:

_____

_____

_____

_____

_____

_____

DATE: __ / __ / __

I AWAKENED TO THIS KNOWLEDGE OF THE WORLD:

_____

_____

_____

_____

_____

_____

If every day is an awakening, you will never grow old. You will just keep growing.

Gail Sheehy

Awaken Your Senses:
Smell

This morn the air smells of vanilla
and oranges.

Ralph Waldo Emerson

DATE: __ / __ / __

This morn the air smells of _____

and _____.

DATE: __ / __ / __

This morning I jump-started my day with an oil, shampoo, lotion, or tea,

scented with:

☐ citrus (for happiness)

☐ peppermint (for concentration)

☐ rosemary (for mental and physical energy)

☐ eucalyptus (for alertness)

☐ _____
other

*Better than any argument is
to rise at dawn
and pick dew-wet red
berries in a cup.*

Wendell Berry

A simple act that gave me pleasure this morning:

_____

_____

_____

_____

_____

I was especially perceptive to all things beautiful that morning—raspberries in blue china bowls were enough to make the heart sing.

Irene Hunt

A simple beauty that made my heart sing this morning:

_____

_____

_____

_____

_____

Dream Catcher

DATE: __ / __ / __

What forgotten thing screamed for help in my dream last night:

_____

_____

_____

_____

_____

_____

_____

_____

All the things one has forgotten scream for help in dreams.

Elias Canetti

DATE: __ / __ / __

How I will handle the thing that screamed out to me in my dream last night:

_____

_____

_____

_____

_____

_____

_____

_____

The mind is most acute and most uneasy in the morning.

Johann von Goethe, attributed

DATE: __ / __ / __

A SIGN OF MY MENTAL ACUTENESS THIS MORNING:

_____

_____

_____

_____

_____

_____

DATE: __ / __ / __

WHAT I AM MOST UNEASY ABOUT THIS MORNING:

_____

_____

_____

_____

_____

_____

Breathing in, I calm my body.
Breathing out, I smile.

Thich Nhat Hanh

How breathing centered me this morning:

_____

_____

_____

_____

_____

THE QUIETER YOU BECOME, THE MORE YOU CAN HEAR.

Ram Dass

What I can hear in the quiet this morning:

_____

_____

_____

_____

_____

DATE: __/__/__

Morning Tip:

Set daily goals.

Before going to bed, write down three or four small goals or tasks for the next day. Review and adjust these goals in the morning. Their accomplishment will give you confidence and move you slowly toward your larger goals.

☐ My small goal for today:

_____

☐ My larger goal:

_____

_____

Let your first hour set the theme of success and positive action that is certain to echo through your entire day.

Og Mandino

My theme of success and positive action today:

_____

_____

_____

_____

_____

If you had half an hour of exercise this morning, you're in the right frame of mind to sit still and focus on this paragraph, and your brain is far more equipped to remember it.

John J. Ratey

After half an hour of exercise this morning, I read and remembered this:

_____

_____

_____

_____

_____

DATE: __ / __ / __

SEE WHAT PROFIT WE GET FROM DAILY EXERCISE.

Seneca the Younger

My exercise this morning:

_____

_____

_____

My profit:

_____

_____

_____

DATE: __ / __ / __

**I WAS EXCITED TO GET UP THIS MORNING AND TRY TO CHANGE
THE WORLD BY:**

_____

_____

_____

_____

_____

_____

DATE: __ / __ / __

**I WAS EXCITED TO GET UP THIS MORNING AND WORK ON THIS
IMPORTANT THING:**

_____

_____

_____

_____

_____

_____

If you're changing the world, you're working on important things. You're excited to get up in the morning.

Larry Page

Thank You!
Thank You!
Thank You!

Thankfulness is the beginning
of gratitude. Gratitude is the
completion of thankfulness.
Thankfulness may consist merely
of words. Gratitude is shown in acts.

Henri Frédéric Amiel

DATE: __ / __ / __

My words of thankfulness this morning:

_____

_____

_____

_____

_____

DATE: __ / __ / __

My act of gratitude this morning:

_____

_____

_____

_____

_____

I can never decide whether my dreams are the result of my thoughts, or my thoughts are the result of my dreams.

D. H. Lawrence

My _____ was
dream/thought

the result of this _____:
dream/thought

_____

_____

_____

_____

_____

THE BEST WAY TO MAKE YOUR DREAMS COME TRUE IS TO WAKE UP.

Paul Valéry

When I woke up, I accomplished this:

_____

_____

_____

_____

_____

MORNING ROUTINE

I wake up about 4:00 A.M. and I get out of bed, shave,
and then I work out for about an hour and a half. . . .
I've learned that if I don't follow my morning routine,
my mood is influenced. I look at the clock to see when
I can work out; my body expects certain things at certain
times, and I find if I don't do them I just don't feel
physically right.

General Stanley McChrystal

How I feel when I don't follow my morning routine:

_____

_____

_____

_____

_____

How you spend your morning can often tell you what kind of day you are going to have.

Lemony Snicket

How I spent my morning:

_____

_____

_____

_____

_____

I expect my day to be: ☐ productive   ☐ stressful

☐ unproductive   ☐ happy

☐ calm   ☐ unhappy

As we arise each morning, let us determine to respond with love and kindness to whatever might come our way.

Thomas S. Monson

DATE: __ / __ / __

LOVE I DETERMINE TO SHOW TODAY:

_____

_____

_____

_____

_____

_____

DATE: __ / __ / __

KINDNESS I DETERMINE TO SHOW TODAY:

_____

_____

_____

_____

_____

_____

Set wide the window.
Let me drink the day.

Edith Wharton

This morning I opened the window and felt:

_____

_____

_____

_____

_____

Outside the window
The morning air is all awash
with angels.

Richard Wilbur

The "angels" outside my window this morning:

_____

_____

_____

_____

_____

M-E-D-I-T-A-T-E:

Coffee

Once you've poured your coffee into a mug, begin to engage your
senses. Look at the deep color and the movement of the liquid.
Watch the steam rise. Now close your eyes. Inhale the warm mist and the
aroma. Cradle the mug, feeling the warmth enter your hands. Take a sip.
Feel the sensations and flavor in your mouth and in your throat:
warmth, thickness, tanginess, richness.

☐ I did it!

☐ How I feel:

_____

DATE: __ / __ / __

The morning cup of coffee has an exhilaration about it which the cheering influence of the afternoon or evening cup of tea cannot be expected to reproduce.

Oliver Wendell Holmes Sr.

What I did this morning, exhilarated by my cup of coffee:

_____

_____

_____

_____

_____

_____

It was morning; through the high window
I saw the pure, bright blue of the sky as it
hovered cheerfully over the long roofs of the
neighboring houses. It too seemed full of joy,
as if it had special plans, and had put on its
finest clothes for the occasion.

Hermann Hesse, attributed

My special plan this morning for a joyous day:

_____

_____

_____

_____

_____

DATE: __ / __ / __

When you arise in the morning,
think on what a precious privilege
it is to live–to breathe–to think–
to enjoy–to love!

Marcus Aurelius

I feel grateful this morning for the privilege of:

_____

_____

_____

_____

_____

DATE: __ / __ / __

THIS MORNING I DECIDED TO SAVE THE WORLD BY:

_____

_____

_____

_____

_____

_____

DATE: __ / __ / __

THIS MORNING I DECIDED TO SAVOR THE WORLD BY:

_____

_____

_____

_____

_____

_____

A friend told me that each morning when we get up we have to decide whether we are going to save or savor the world. I don't think that is the decision. It's not an either/or. . . . We have to do both, save *and* savor the world.

Kate Clinton

Awaken Your Senses:
Taste

Sour, sweet, bitter, pungent,
all must be tasted.

Chinese proverb

DATE: __ / __ / __

My first tastes of the morning:

- ☐ sour: _____
- ☐ sweet: _____
- ☐ bitter: _____
- ☐ pungent: _____

DATE: __ / __ / __

My favorite taste this morning:

_____

_____

_____

_____

_____

_____

I love waking up without an alarm . . . . a signal that something is not right . . . ensuring that we emerge from sleep in full fight-or-flight mode, flooded with stress hormones and adrenaline as our body readies itself for danger.

Arianna Huffington

My waking face:

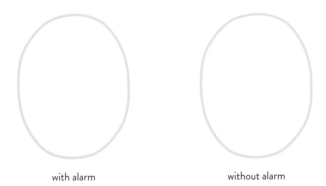

with alarm   without alarm

DATE: __ / __ / __

MORNING COMES WHETHER YOU SET THE ALARM OR NOT.

Ursula K. Le Guin

What woke me up this morning:

_____

_____

_____

_____

_____

Dream Catcher

DATE: __ / __ / __

This was insane in my dream last night:

_____

_____

_____

_____

_____

_____

_____

_____

Dreaming permits each and every one of us to be quietly and safely insane every night of our lives.

William Dement

Draw a wild and crazy scene from your dream last night.

I HAVE HEARD THE
MAVIS SINGING
ITS LOVE-SONG
TO THE MORN;
I'VE SEEN THE
DEW-DROP CLINGING
TO THE ROSE JUST
NEWLY BORN.

Charles Jeffreys

DATE: __ / __ / __

THIS MORNING I HEARD:

_____

_____

_____

_____

_____

_____

DATE: __ / __ / __

THIS MORNING I SAW:

_____

_____

_____

_____

_____

DON'T PUT OFF TILL TOMORROW WHAT CAN BE ENJOYED TODAY.

Josh Billings

Something I enjoyed the moment I woke up:

_____

_____

_____

_____

_____

Every day you wake up to transcend.

Carlos Santana

How I can transcend today:

_____

_____

_____

_____

_____

Morning Tip:

Don't waste the weekend.

Instead of sleeping late on Saturdays and Sundays, keep to your usual wake-up schedule. Spend those early hours on chores to free up the weekend for fun, exploration, and special projects.

☐ When I woke up this weekend morning: ___:___ A.M.

☐ What I accomplished with my extra hours:

_____

_____

_____

Be in the habit of getting up bright and early on the weekends just the way you do on the weekdays. Why waste such precious time in bed?

Marilyn vos Savant

☐ When I woke up this weekend morning: ___:___ A.M.

☐ Fun I had in my extra hours:

_____

_____

_____

Expect problems and eat them for breakfast.

Alfred A. Montapert, attributed

The problem I will eat for breakfast today:

_____

_____

_____

_____

_____

There was never a night or a problem that could defeat sunrise or hope.

Bernard Williams, attributed

The problem defeated by sunrise or hope this morning:

_____

_____

_____

_____

_____

DATE: __ / __ / __

I SAILED OUT AT SUNRISE ON THIS PERSONAL JOURNEY:

_____

_____

_____

_____

_____

_____

DATE: __ / __ / __

I SAILED OUT AT SUNRISE ON THIS PROFESSIONAL JOURNEY:

_____

_____

_____

_____

_____

_____

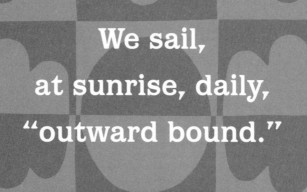

We sail,
at sunrise, daily,
"outward bound."

Helen Hunt Jackson

Morning

DATE: ___ / ___ / ___

Create your own personal affirmation of spirituality by using one of the adjectives below.

I, _____, am _____ and can appreciate
　　your name　　　　　　　*adjective*　　　　　the magic around me.

open

sensitive

curious

grateful

mystic

hopeful

evolving

_____

other

Affirmation
SPIRITUALITY

DATE: __ / __ / __

Write your personal affirmation of spirituality 5 times around this circle.

Mornings come much too early in the day.

Lea Rush

If it were up to me, mornings would begin at ____:____ A.M./P.M.

There should be a rule against
people trying to be funny
before the sun comes up.

Kristen Chandler

I don't speak to anyone or let anyone speak to me until

____:____ A.M./P.M.

MORNING ROUTINE

Prayer is such an important part of my routine—
and probably the only thing, next to coffee, that I never
fail to include. Prayers remind me that today is a gift,
no matter how I use it. . . . Running a mile before
breakfast and Instagramming my avocado toast
isn't necessarily a part of that.

Ana Marie Cox

My prayer of gratitude for the gift of this morning:

_____

_____

_____

_____

_____

Gratitude can transform common days into thanksgivings.

William Arthur Ward,
attributed

How I will transform this common day into a thanksgiving:

_____

_____

_____

_____

_____

I've learned that every day you should reach out and touch someone. People love a warm hug, or just a friendly pat on the back.

Maya Angelou, attributed

DATE: __ / __ / __

FIRST WARM HUG OR FRIENDLY PAT I GAVE THIS MORNING:

_____

_____

_____

_____

_____

_____

DATE: __ / __ / __

FIRST WARM HUG OR FRIENDLY PAT I GOT THIS MORNING:

_____

_____

_____

_____

_____

As soon as you open your eyes in the morning, you can square away for a happy and successful day. It's the mood and the purpose at the inception of each day that are important facts in charting your course for the day.

George Matthew Adams,
attributed

My mood and purpose this morning:

_____

_____

_____

_____

The best things are nearest: breath in your nostrils, light in your eyes, flowers at your feet, duties at your hand.

Robert Louis Stevenson

The best things of my morning:

_____

_____

_____

_____

_____

MORNING
STRETCH

FORWARD FOLD

Sit up erect in bed, with your arms
raised above your head and your
legs straight in front of you. Inhale,
lengthening your spine. Exhale,
bending forward and reaching
toward your feet. Repeat the
breathing, bending further and
further forward with each exhale.
When you reach your limit,
relax your neck and take 10 deep
breaths. Slowly stretch back up.

☐ I did it this morning!
☐ I will do this again.

IF ANYTHING IS SACRED, THE HUMAN BODY IS SACRED.

Walt Whitman

How I honored my body this morning:

_____

_____

_____

_____

_____

A day dawns, quite like other days; in it, a single hour comes, quite like other hours; but in that day and in that hour the chance of a lifetime faces us.

Maltbie D. Babcock

The chance this morning showed me:

_____

_____

_____

_____

_____

The moment when first you wake up in the morning is the most wonderful of the twenty-four hours. No matter how weary or dreary you may feel, you possess the certainty that . . . absolutely anything may happen. And the fact that it practically always *doesn't*, matters not one jot. The possibility is always there.

Monica Baldwin

Today's wonderful possibility:

_____

_____

_____

_____

DATE: __ / __ / __

HOW MY MORNING HABITS CONTRIBUTE TO MY HEALTH:

_____

_____

_____

DATE: __ / __ / __

HOW MY MORNING HABITS CONTRIBUTE TO MY WEALTH:

_____

_____

_____

DATE: __ / __ / __

HOW MY MORNING HABITS CONTRIBUTE TO MY WISDOM:

_____

_____

_____

It is also well
to be up before
daybreak, for such
habits contribute
to health, wealth,
and wisdom.

Aristotle

Thank You!
Thank You!
Thank You!

"Thank you" is the best prayer that
anyone could say. I say that one
a lot. "Thank you" expresses
extreme gratitude, humility,
understanding.

Alice Walker

DATE: __ / __ / __

Dear _____ ,

Thank you for

_____

_____

_____

_____

_____

DATE: __ / __ / __

Dear _____ ,

Thank you for

_____

_____

_____

_____

_____

The person who doesn't scatter the morning dew will not comb gray hairs.

Irish proverb

How I scattered the morning dew:

_____

_____

_____

_____

_____

Today is the first day of the rest of your life.

Abbie Hoffman

How I started the first day of the rest of my life:

_____

_____

_____

_____

_____

Dream Catcher

DATE: __ / __ / __

Yes! The boring dream I had last night:

_____

_____

_____

_____

_____

_____

_____

_____

Did anyone ever have a boring dream?

Ralph Hodgson

DATE: __ / __ / __

A fascinating dream I had last night (draw or describe):

I LIVE A DAY AT A TIME. EACH DAY I LOOK FOR A KERNEL OF EXCITEMENT. IN THE MORNING, I SAY: "WHAT IS MY EXCITING THING FOR TODAY?"

Barbara Jordan

DATE: __ / __ / __

MY PERSONAL KERNEL OF EXCITEMENT THIS MORNING:

_____

_____

_____

_____

_____

_____

DATE: __ / __ / __

MY PROFESSIONAL KERNEL OF EXCITEMENT THIS MORNING:

_____

_____

_____

_____

_____

_____

Morning Tip:

Work on a personal passion project.

Carve out a modest chunk of time in the morning (15 minutes to an hour)
for a personal project unrelated to work. Learn a language, sing scales,
research family history, paint, or . . .

My personal passion project:

_____

_____

_____

Early in the morning, at break of day, in all the freshness and dawn of one's strength, to read a book—I call that vicious!

Friedrich Nietzsche

Early in the morning to do this: _____,

I call that vicious!

Let us, then, be up and doing,
With a heart for any fate.

Henry Wadsworth Longfellow

I got up at ____:____ A.M.

This is what I am doing:

_____

_____

_____

_____

_____

The lark is up to meet the sun,
The bee is on the wing,
The ant his labor has begun,
The woods with music ring.
Shall bird and bee and ant be wise
While I my moments waste?

William McGuffey

Shall bird and bee and ant be wise while I my moments waste?

☐ yes

☐ no

And with all the pent-up love of my heart,
I bid you the top o' the mornin'.

John Locke

I bid these people the top o' the mornin' today:

_____

_____

_____

_____

_____

_____

MEASURE YOUR MORNINGS

NOW, after 365 days of meaningful mornings, how well do your early hours brighten your prospect for days of health, energy, achievement, peace, goodness, and joy?

Mark the brightness of your internal sun today.

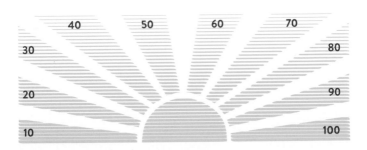

ISBN 978-0-593-13746-8

Printed in China

Conceived and compiled by Dian G. Smith and Robie Rogge
Book design by Nicole Block
Illustrations by Christopher David Ryan

10 9 8 7 6 5 4 3 2 1

First Edition